This book belongs

Paperback ISBN: 978-1-63731-866-9
Hardcover ISBN: 978-1-63731-868-3
eBook ISBN: 978-1-63731-867-6

Printed and bound in the USA.
NinjaLifeHacks.tv

Ninja Life Hacks®
by Mary Nhin

The dragon dances, through streets we roam,
From house to house, we happily comb.
Gongs and cheers fill the air,
The New Year's joy is everywhere!

My shyness melts, fears fly away,
In the dragon dance, I find my way.
With each twirl and each sway,
I embrace my shy, timid display.

Chinese Zodiac Sign

Rooster
1981, 1993, 2005, 2017

Dog
1982, 1994, 2006, 2018

Pig
1983, 1995, 2007, 2019

Rat
1984, 1996, 2008, 2020

Ox
1985, 1997, 2009, 2021

Tiger
1986, 1998, 2010, 2022

Rabbit
1987, 1999, 2011, 2023

Dragon
1988, 2000, 2012, 2024

Snake
1989, 2001, 2013, 2025

Horse
1990, 2002, 2014, 2026

Goat
1991, 2003, 2015, 2027

Monkey
1992, 2004, 2016, 2028

Remembering the **F.U.N.** method could be your secret weapon when fear strikes!

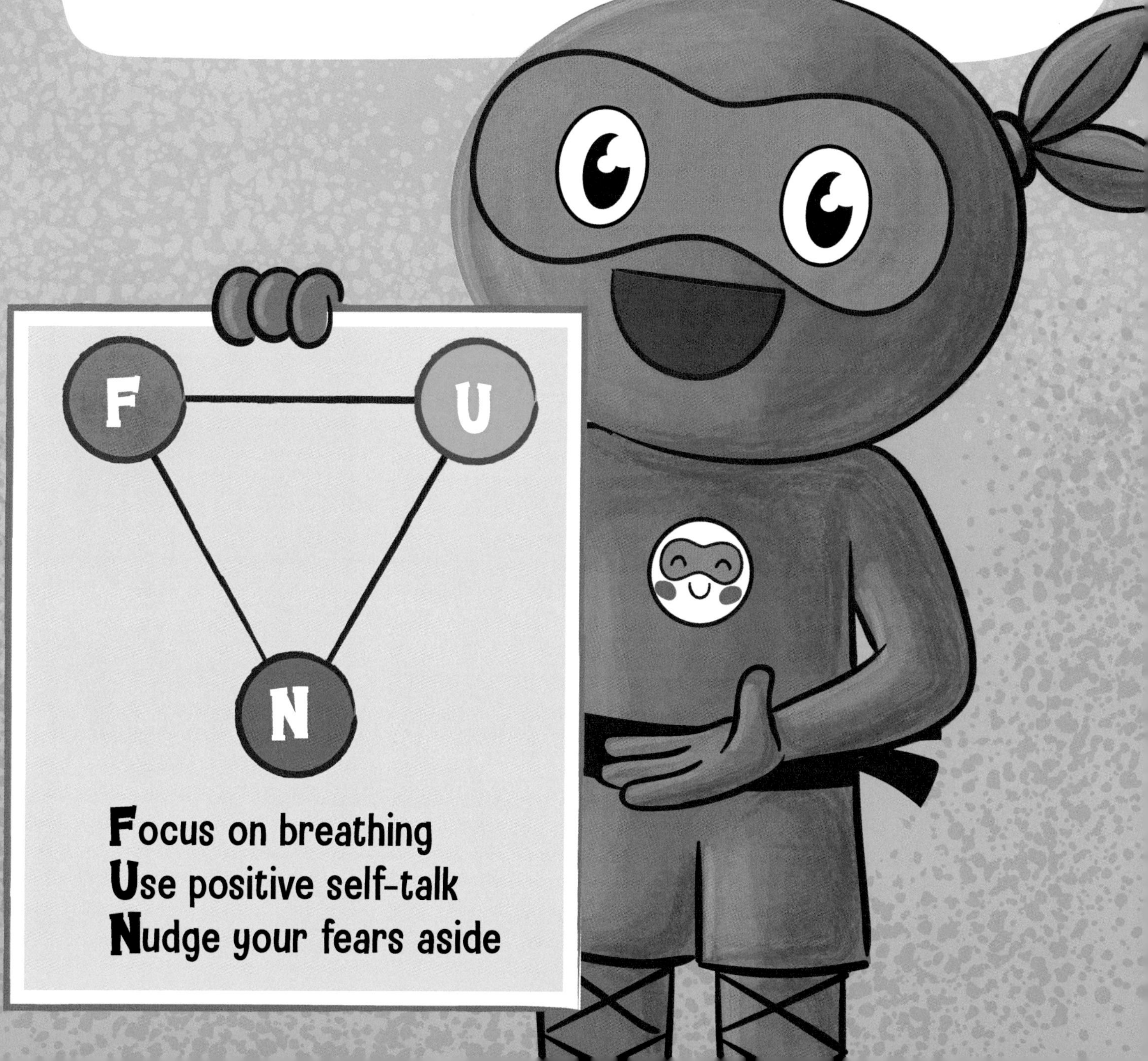

Check out all the **F.U.N.** in the Lunar New Year lesson plans which include STEM activities, printables, worksheets, crafts, and coloring sheets at ninjalifehacks.tv!

I love to hear from my readers.
Write to me at info@ninjalifehacks.tv or send me mail at:

Mary Nhin
6608 N Western Avenue #1166
Oklahoma City, OK 73116

 @officialninjalifehacks

 Mary Nhin   Ninja Life Hacks

 @marynhin @officialninjalifehacks
#NinjaLifeHacks

 Ninja Life Hacks

88273748R10021